Wonderful
WORDS:

Fun Poems About Words
(for Kids or Anyone Who's a Kid at Heart)

by **Mary E. Kendig**

To order additional copies of this book, contact:
Xlibris
844-714-8691
www.Xlibris.com
Orders@Xlibris.com

ISBN: Softcover   978-1-4134-9678-9
        EBook   978-1-6641-3746-2

Library of Congress Control Number: 2005904655

Print information available on the last page

Rev. date: 10/14/2020

For Jerry and Mom,
and all the kids I know (big and small!),
with love and thanks for your constant inspiration.

ACKNOWLEDGMENTS

Thanks also to my friends and family members
for their help, encouragement, and support
in writing this book of poems.

Poems and Illustrations by Mary E. Kendig

MOM is **WOW**!

If ever I am feeling down,
if ever my smile becomes a frown,
MOM is there to turn it around.
Much more than just your average noun,
MOM is **WOW** turned upside down!
These thoughts are echoed and
world-renowned.

No matter what city, province, or town,
MOM's the best lady ever found —
MOM is **WOW** turned upside down!

A Daughter Equals Laughter

A daughter is a treasure,
the sweetest thoughts she does compel.
She's a giving, caring person,
as most anyone can tell.
A daughter is a miracle,
and one thought you can't dispel:
A daughter equals laughter —
just replace the D with L!

Dad Once Was a Lad

Before DAD was DAD,
he once was a lad.
He's a boy who grew up,
and made his folks glad,
(well, except for the few times
he made 'em both mad!)

But boys will be boys —
it isn't a fad,
sometimes they're happy,
and sometimes they're sad.
At times, they are good,
and at other times, bad.

Remind you of someone?
A lass or a lad
who takes after the man
he or she calls a DAD?

In the circle of life,
during good times and bad,
by your side through the years,
you'll be glad to have had
the lad who grew up
and became dear old DAD.

To a Son, Rising

When a son is smiling,
he's like a song.
With a song in his heart,
so sweetly he'll sing.
When a son sings sweetly,
he is as a bird.
And, just as a bird,
he will one day take wing.

When a son takes wing,
he will find he can fly.
Propelled by discovery,
he'll fly to the sky.
On reaching the sky,
his quest not yet done —
He'll rise even higher, on his way
to the sun.

One to Sixteen

ONE day, I won a prize —
I wished to share it with TWO friends.
The prize was THREE free meals for FOUR
at the midtown Rainbow's End.
The Rainbow's End is a restaurant
that's down on FIVE Palms Road.
So at SIX o'clock, from SEVENTH Street
to the restaurant we rode.
I ate EIGHT ravioli,
and my friend ate NINE (one more),
and my other friend had TEN fried shrimp —
never ate so much before!
My brother, he ate with us, too,
then drove us to a show.
When it got to be ELEVEN,
it was time for us to go.
We bought a dozen cookies (that's TWELVE!)
as an extra-special treat,
and traveled back to my house,
1314 Springfield Street.
FIFTEEN minutes later,
my special day was through.
Hope YOU have a special day
when YOU turn SIXTEEN, too!

THERE to WHERE? to HERE!

There

One letter makes the difference,
to get from HERE to THERE.
The T could stand for Travel,
which is how to get somewhere.
But if you're THERE, WHERE are
you?

Where?

You're just a letter away:
The T becomes the W,
which helps you find your way!
And once you're WHERE you want to be,
you've come from far to near.
When you travel back from WHERE you
were,
your trip's complete —
you're HERE!

Here!

What rhymes with... Jerry?

I Know . . .

I know a Mary
who's not so contrary,
and I know a Carlos
who's sweet.
And I know a Rose —
loved wherever she goes,
and I know an Adam
who's neat.
I know a Billy
who acts kinda silly,
and I think he likes me a lot.
And I know a Jerry,
a Jane, and a Terry,
and they're the best friends
that I've got.

Now, think of the friends
who are special to you,
and try making rhymes
with their names.
I know you'll like to
as much as I do —
it's one of my
favorite games!

Big Uncle Pete and Little Auntie Pat

Big Uncle Pete,
who's pretty neat,
really, really loves to eat.
My Auntie Pat,
she isn't fat.
I'd say she's tiny, or petite.
She often tells
my Uncle Pete
to find some better
things to eat
like bulgur wheat,
and beans, and beets
(She wishes he would
cut out sweets)
and strange foods,
like pig's feet!

Big Uncle Pete,
well, he loves meat.
To him, rare steak
is such a treat.
Yet, Auntie Pat
won't go for that.
She'd rather eat
her old straw hat!

They don't agree
on what to eat,
but Pete loves Pat,
and Pat loves Pete.
Each half makes
the whole complete.
And I love 'em both —
they're really neat,
'cause no matter what
they like to eat,
they're Auntie Pat
and Uncle Pete!

For My Friends

Fun times, and laughter, and just being ther

Remembering moments together.

Ice cream, and daydreams, and promises mac

Even a few storms to weather.

Never a burden and always a joy,

Dear Friend, hope you're my Friend forever

For My Family

Finding my way in this world can be hard,

Always helps to have loved ones to lean on.

Mindful protectors who guide me along,

Inspiring me daily to keep on,

Life is so special because you are near,

You're the ones who allow me to dream on!

Ark, It's an Oodle!

ARK, ARK, add an M
on your MARK, get set:
Remove the M and add a B —
BARK is what you get.
Remove the B and add a P,
PARK is your new word.
Remove the P — you're back, you see,
to the first word that you heard!

OODLE, OODLE, add a D
DOODLE's what you get.
Remove the D and add a P —
a POODLE is your pet!
Remove the P and add an N,
NOODLE is the word.
Remove the N — you're back again,
to the first word that you heard!

n

_oodle

b

p

d

_ark

m

Q: So, does ANYTHING rhyme with purple or orange?
A: Well, not exactly, but you can come close!

Ode to Orange and Purple (and bein' a kid)

I'm certain that you will forage
in search of a juicy orange,
unless you find something better,
like chocolate, along the way!

And if the drink is purple,
I'm sure that you will slurp 'til
all the juice has vanished,
and your teeth start to decay!

To be a kid is great, indeed.
Sweet treats seem to abound
(that is, until that "figure
of authority" comes around. . . .)

Add a Letter, Lose a Letter
(Can you guess the word?)
(See answers at end!)

A
An ANT's a really small but busy creature, you see,
but add a U — you've got a member of your family tree!

B
A BIT is a wee portion of the smallest degree,
but add an A — it's what you use to catch a fish in the sea!

C
CARE is what you show when you help anyone in need,
but lose the E — it's how you travel from Point A to Point B!

D
A DINER's where you go if you want something neat to eat,
but lose the R — it's what you do there — now, isn't that a treat!

E
EVE could stand for *evening* or could be a girl's first name,
but add an N and it's odd's opposite in the numbers game!

F
FAR describes a distance that's not terribly near,
but add an E to pay the cabby so that she can get you here!

G

A GOAT's a cool farm animal, could even be a pet,
but lose the A — you've got a verb that is the past tense of *get!*

H

HALT means stop completely at the light if it's red,
but lose the L — it's what you wear to warm the top of your head!

I

IN's a preposition — it's the opposite of *out,*
but add an N and it's a place to stay when traveling about!

J

JET is something big that you see flying through the clouds,
but add an S and it's an act that causes laughter — sometimes loud!

K

KIND means being good of heart to everyone you see,
but lose the D and it's a word that's slang for someone's family!

L

LOST is what you are if you just can't find your way,
but lose the S and it's a place where you play baseball every day!

M

A MAN is what a boy grows up to be, eventually,
but add a Y and it's a word that means a massive quantity!

N
A NET is something used to catch a fish or butterfly,
but add an S and it's a home for birds before they learn to fly!

O
ONCE could stand for something that has happened in the past,
but lose the C — it means a single thing — now, isn't that a blast?

P
PAINT's applied to walls to make things look their very best,
but lose the I — it's what a dog does when it's really out of breath!

Q
QUIT means to end something if you choose to, or to stop,
but add an E — it means so free of noise that you can hear a pin drop!

R
READ is what you're doing now, as you review this rhyme,
but add a Y — it means you're willing and prepared at any time!

S
SHORE is a vacation spot where you can "beat the heat,"
but lose the R and it's an item into which you put your feet!

T
A TALLY is a score you keep, like maybe for a sport,
but lose the Y and it's a word that means the opposite of *short!*

U

A UNIT is a portion — a small part of something bigger,
but add an E — it means to merge, or to bring something together!

V

A VAT's a giant tub, and liquid's usually stored inside,
but add an S and it describes a stretch of land that's big and wide!

W

WEST is a direction on a map or weather vane,
but lose the S — it's what you get when you are standing in the rain!

X

An X-RAY is a scan that doctors use to see what's wrong,
but lose the X and it's a beam of light that's really bright and strong!

Y

YARN is what you use to knit a soft and cuddly warm thing.
Add an E and it's a word that means to wish or long for something!

Z

A ZOO's a place where you can see a lion or giraffe,
but add an M and it's the noise you hear when you go really fast!

ANSWERS:

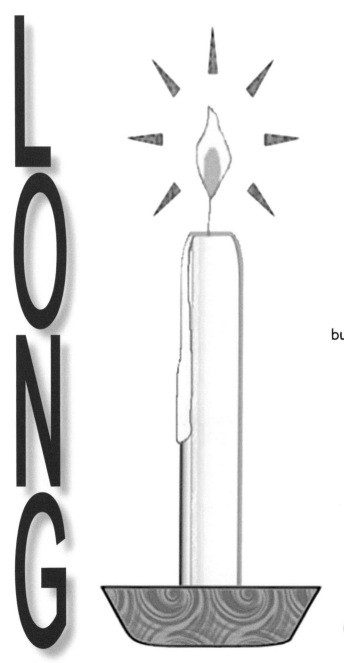

The Long and Short of It

Sometimes, the same old letter
makes quite a different sound,
depending on just one thing:
the word in which it's found!

Take *living,* for example,
and think of *giving,* too.
Now pay really close attention,
and watch what the *i* can do!

Say *diving* or *surviving.*
It's still the same old *i,*
but the sound has gone from short to long —
now give these words a try:

Say *foot* or *soot,* for instance.
These have a double *o,*
but the double *o's* sound different
in some other words you know!

Say *boot* or *root* or *hoot* or *toot.*
You'll hear another sound.
The *o's* have gone from short to long —
let's try another round!

■ ■ ■ ■ ■

Consider words like *car* or *mad*
the *a's* aren't quite the same,
or how 'bout words like *far* or *fad* —
watch how these words can change:

Just take the end, tack on an *e,*
for *fade* or *made* or *care.*
The *a* sound goes from short to long —
you've got four new words there!

Now take some words with vowels in them,
like *a, e, i, o, u,*
compare the sounds and listen
to just what those letters do!

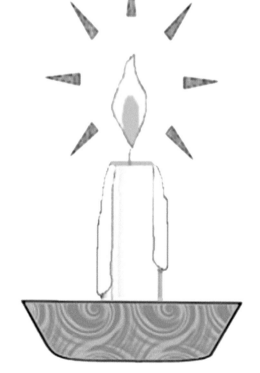

SHORT

Immeasurable Fun . . .

We took a drive through winding roads,
saw mountains, lakes, and flowers.
No special reason for our trip —
took only a few hours.

Several cars rode past us
as we made our way along.
We joked a bunch, laughed a lot,
and sang some traveling songs.

We must've gone a hundred miles,
past thousands of tall trees.
Dad opened a car window,
so that we could feel the breeze.

We rode along a giant lake,
saw water everywhere!
I asked, "How many gallons
of lake water are in there?"

"At least hundreds of thousands"
was Dad's rather quick reply.
"About as many stars as
you can see up in the sky!"

"No," I said, "there's gotta be
a million stars up there!
'Cause at night, if you look up,
you see them shining everywhere!"

Dad laughed and said, "You're right!
I should just call you 'little scholar'!"
(No, I wouldn't trade this road trip
even for a billion dollars!)

As we turned for home, I realized
that the fun times just like these
add up to an endless number
of the fondest memories!

Preposition Park

The prepositions in this poem are in blue . . . .

(Prepositions are connector words like *of, by, on,* and *around* —
They connect phrases to other words like verbs and nouns.)

Shel and her mom walked up several blocks
to meet with Shel's friend at the giant rock.
They spotted a neighbor along the way,
who said to them both, "Have a pleasant day!"
The neighbor's old dog even barked "Hello!"
"Wish I could talk, but I've gotta go,"
shouted Shel in a hurry above the noise
made by some of the neighborhood girls and boys.
Shel looked at her watch, waved so long,
and said to her mom, "Must be moving along!"
Under the bridge and over the hill,
beyond the town square, and past the mill
toward the park, they made their way —
was a wonderful walk on a rather brisk day.
Charlotte, her friend, was there near the rock,
standing right by the fence as Shel rounded the block.
Into the park, Shel started to scurry
(now out of breath, as she was still in a hurry).
Char greeted Shel with a hug and a smile,
and they laughed as they played at the park for a while.
Char's sis was there, too, and Charlotte's dog, Clay,
who got into the fun catching frisbees all day!
They enjoyed a fine day among birds and flowers —
in fact, the whole gang spent about seven hours
having quite a great time at Preposition Park.
Then they all said goodbye and got home before dark!

2 + 2 = Something New!

INSTRUCTIONS:
Use adjectives (descriptive words) that have three or more syllables (parts).

Take the first two parts of the first word,

and the second two parts of the second word,
and make a new word!
Do this four times if you can,
and then use your four new words in a rhyme!

Here's one try at it; let's see what YOU can do!

Fabulous + Delicious = Fabulicious
Stupendous + Incredible = Stupendible
Exciting + Entertaining = Excitaining
Beautiful + Magnificent = Beautificent

A fabulicious time was had today,
it was simply stupendible in every way.
The things we did were so excitaining,
a beautificent day — though it ended up raining!

$$\begin{array}{r} \overset{1}{m}\overset{2}{arvelous} \\ + \;\; \overset{1}{f}\overset{2}{antastic} \\ \hline marveltastic! \end{array}$$

Sidney the Goat

Sidney's the name of my pet goat,
whose diet is mostly of grains, like oat.
Sid drinks so much water, you'd think he'd float
on the waves at sea, as if he were a boat!
Now, I'm usually not inclined to gloat,
but my Sidney is like no other goat:
His hair has such a shiny coat,
I've heard other goat owners say (and I quote):
"Just look at the coat on that big old goat!"
But the chance that they'll find their own
Sidney's remote,
'cause there's no goat like Sidney —
and that's all she wrote!

What Makes a Sentence?
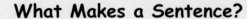
(A rhyme about nouns > verbs > adjectives > adverbs)

Nouns are words like *book* or *kite*
or things like *tree* or *house*.
Sometimes, they're things that live and breathe,
like *dog*, or *cat*, or *mouse*.
Nouns are places — people, too,
like *mom* or *sister* dear,
or *brother*, who is living
in a *city* far from here.
Proper nouns are people's names,
like *Smith*, or *Jones*, or *Jane*,
or sites like great *Mount Fuji*,
or U.S. states, like *Maine*.
Nouns also answer questions,
like Where? or What? or Who?
But nouns need verbs in sentences
to show what they can do!

Action verbs are words like *go*,
or *run*, or *play*, or *find*,
but verbs like *be*, *appear*, or *seem* —
they're called the linking kind.
And sometimes, verbs have helpers,
like *is*, or *has*, or *have*.
You can form verbs like *is running*,
have been playing, or *has had!*
These are called verb phrases —
they convey the different tenses.
And when verbs are paired with nouns,
well, they form the core of sentences!

Adjectives are words like *great,*
or *big,* or *mean,* or *nice.*
These words describe such things as nouns:
like *nice dogs* or *big mice!*
Adjectives make thoughts exact.
They add some color, too.
For instance, it's an adjective
that says my *kite is blue!*
And some may answer questions,
such as What kind? or Which one?
For instance, we'd say *my house*
or *that big tree* or *great fun!*
And last, the words *a, an,* and *the*
are special on our list:
These adjectives are articles,
and only three exist!

Adverbs are describing words
that work with verbs like *go.*
Most adverbs end in *–ly.*
There are many that you know!
Slowly, quickly, happily,
are three, to name a few,
so if you have a noun and verb,
here's what you can do:

Take an adverb, any one
and place it near your verb.
Add an adjective for fun
and a connector word.
Then, you'll have a sentence
that's clever and complete,
like this one, for example,
which I think is really neat:

Jane played happily **at my house!**
(noun)-(verb)-(adverb)-(connector)-(adjective)-(noun)

So, if YOU connect some words like mine
you'll see a sentence come alive —
With nouns, verbs, and supporting words
just think of what YOU can describe!

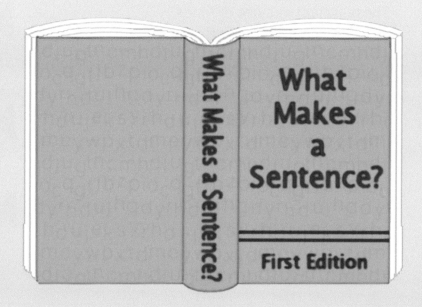

What Makes a Sentence?

What
Makes
a
Sentence?

First Edition

How Do People Say HELLO?

What do you say when you meet someone new
who doesn't speak quite like you do?
To learn a short greeting that they'll
understand,
just remember these words, as I do!

In English, it's typically "Hi!" or "Hello!"
In Italian, it's usually "Ciao!"
In French, it's "Salut!" and in Spanish, "Hola!"
In Chinese, it's always "Ni hao!"

If Japan is your home, you say "Konnichiwa!"
If it's Germany, it's "Guten Tag!"

In Swedish, it's "Hej," in Norwegian, "Hallo!"
In Hawaii, you say, "Aloha!"

In parts of West Africa, you say "Fofo!"
And in Russian, it could be "Preevyet!"
In Turkish, "Merhaba," in Hebrew, "Shalom!"
In Tibet, you say "Tashi Delek!"

From this simple beginning, you can go far,
so just practice these words and you'll find
that learning a language
is really quite fun
if you take it one word at a time!

Similar **but** Different

Have you ever come across a word that seems to have a mate,
and the two words are so similar, it's hard to keep them straight?

Like *SIT* and *SET*, for instance, or words like *RAISE* and *RISE*?
Or how 'bout words like *TO* and *TOO*, or even *LAY* and *LIE?*

This rhyme may come in handy for pairs of words like these.
If you memorize this poem, then those words will be a breeze!

SIT is what a person does reclining in a chair,
at the theater for a movie, or outdoors, for some fresh air.
When you *SET* something, like cups and plates, you're placing them
somewhere,
like on the kitchen table, when you have dinner there.

RAISE means to lift something high, as when you *RAISE* your hand,
or when you lift your voice to sing if you are in a band.
RISE means simply to come up, like bread does when it bakes,
or like the sun does in the sky each morning as you wake.

*TO'*s a preposition (which you've heard about before!)
You use it when you tell someone you're going *TO* the store.
TOO sounds just like *TO* but means "as well" or "in addition,"
with a little something extra — that's the *O* in repetition!

LAY means to put something down, like carpet on a floor
or when you *LAY* a pen down if you can't write anymore!
LIE means to recline or rest, as to *LIE* down in bed,
and gently have your favorite fluffy pillow meet your head.

So if you see pair of words that seem alike to you,
remember that this simple rhyme can be a little clue.

Words are just like flowers, and this we know is true:
They have some things in common, but they are different, too!

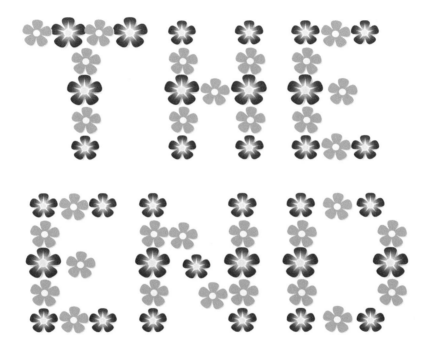

Printed in the United States
By Bookmasters